APR 2 9 2011

MERE ENVIRONMENTALISM

A BIBLICAL PERSPECTIVE ON HUMANS
AND THE NATURAL WORLD

WITHDRAWN

D1166964

ONONDAGA COUNTY PUBLIC LIBRARY
THE GALLERIES OF SYRACUSE
447 SOUTH SALINA ST.
SYRACUSE, NY 13202-2494

MERE ENVIRONMENTALISM

A BIBLICAL PERSPECTIVE ON HUMANS AND THE NATURAL WORLD

Steven F. Hayward

AEI Press
Publisher for the American Enterprise Institute
Washington, D.C.

Distributed by arrangement with the National Book Network
15200 NBN Way, Blue Ridge Summit, PA 17214
To order call toll free 1-800-462-6420 or 1-717-794-3800.

For all other inquiries please contact AEI Press, 1150 17th Street, N.W.,
Washington, D.C. 20036 or call 1-800-862-5801.

Copyright © 2011 by the American Enterprise Institute for Public
Policy Research, Washington, D.C.

ALL RIGHTS RESERVED.

Cover Design by Amy Duty and Justin Mezzell
Interior design by Amy Duty, Justin Mezzell, and Jesse Penico

No part of this publication may be used or reproduced in any manner whatsoever without permission in writing from the American
Enterprise Institute except in the case of brief quotations embodied
in news articles, critical articles, or reviews. The views expressed in
the publications of the American Enterprise Institute are those of the
authors and do not necessarily reflect the views of the staff, advisory
panels, officers, or trustees of AEI.

LCCN: 2010028984
ISBN-13: 978-0-8447-4374-5
eISBN-13: 978-0-8447-4375-2

CONTENTS

FOREWORD

by Jay W. Richards

As a child, I spent many summers at a Christian camp in the mountains of New Mexico. The dense forests of pine and spruce trees, cold mountain streams, verdant meadows festooned with wildflowers, and towering Rocky Mountains helped instill in me a love and awe for God's creation. It was there, in the thin air seven thousand feet above sea level, that I first saw a hazy white band of light across the night sky. Only later did I learn that I was peering into the star-dense center of our Milky Way galaxy, thousands of light years away. Perhaps as a result of these formative experiences, I have always seen the creation as one of the ways that God reveals himself to us.

The Bible itself says as much. "From the creation of the world," the Apostle Paul wrote to the church in Rome, "God's invisible qualities, his eternal power and divine nature, have been clearly seen from the things that have been made" (Romans 1:20). And Psalm 19 says that the "heavens declare the glory of God." Theologians have described the creation as "general revelation," whereas Scripture is "special revelation." Now Jews and Christians obviously hold that special revelation in high regard. But if the creation is God's general revelation of himself, how could they not treat it, too, with respect?

For those who revere Scripture, then, environmental stewardship should be a no-brainer. Or so it has always seemed to me. So it came as a surprise when I learned in college that some academics, such as Lynn White, have claimed just the opposite. White famously blamed biblical teaching about God and man as the source of "environmental degradation"; and his argument has been repeated ad nauseam in environmental ethics courses ever since.

Other critics have suggested, similarly, that because Christians believe Christ will return and consummate his kingdom at some point, Christians will tend to disregard the environment. For years, the media spread a story about James Watt, Secretary of the Interior from 1981–83, which seemed to illustrate this problem. Watt, an evangelical Christian, was once asked by a congressional committee whether his views on the end times led him to give the environment short shrift. His real but rarely reported answer was unobjectionable, even commonsensical from a Christian point of view: "I do not know how many future generations we can count on before the Lord returns; whatever it is we have to manage with a skill to leave the resources needed for future generations." This answer did not fit the stereotype, however, so for years, the media often claimed that Watt had said: "After the last tree is felled, Christ will come back." This is now widely known to be apocryphal, but the fact that the slander against Watt persisted for so long suggests that many people think Christian theology is antagonistic to environmental concerns.

As Steven F. Hayward admirably demonstrates in the following pages, this stereotype is baseless. While those who look to the Bible for guidance do not always fully understand or live up to the standards they profess, the Bible is a rich source for environmental ethics. It also provides a stable foundation for assessing environmental concerns with an open mind while avoiding the extremes so characteristic of public debates over the environment.

The relationship between man and nature is hardly a secondary theme in Scripture. On the very first page, in the book of Genesis, the Bible teaches our responsibility over our natural environment. In the great creation epic of Genesis 1, God creates everything over the course of one divine workweek. On the sixth day, God creates human beings, after he has created the other land animals. But human beings, unlike everything else in creation, are created in God's "image." And the image-bearers of God are immediately commanded: "Be fruitful and multiply, and fill the earth and subdue it; have dominion over the fish of the sea and over the birds of the air and over every living thing that moves upon the earth" (Genesis 1:28).

White and others have read this passage superficially, and so confused "dominion" with "domination." But the text is describing the rule of benevolent stewards who represent the good God to the rest of his creation, not tyrants who rape and pillage the countryside at their discretion. As stewards, we're responsible for how we treat and use the environment. In fact, though the word "stewardship" is now common parlance in mainstream environmental discussions, the idea is derived from Scripture.

The biblical picture of how human beings relate to the environment defies the extremes so common in the environmental debate. We are part of God's good creation, as well as its crowning achievement. On the first five days of creation, God looked at what he had done, and pronounced it "good." On the sixth day, however, "God saw everything that he had made," says Genesis, "and indeed, it was very good" (Genesis 1:31).

This biblical idea of stewardship differs from the view of those contemporary environmentalists who would prefer as little human contact with the environment as possible. The Bible claims that God intends for us to use and transform the natural world around us for good purposes. Adam and Eve were put in a garden before the fall, and told to "tend and watch over it" (Genesis 2:15). Working and transforming the Earth, then, is part of God's original blessing, not a curse. The Fall simply turned work into toil, since the ground would resist our efforts to cultivate it.

The biblical perspective is hopeful but realistic. God made the world good, but that world is now fallen. As fallen creatures in a fallen world, we can and do mess things up. We can and do pollute. We can and do act irresponsibly, ignoring the unintended but bad consequences of our actions. Sometimes those actions call for us to change our habits; sometimes they call for a public policy solution.

These insights are easily distilled from the biblical narrative, but only in the last few decades has the "environment" become an abiding ethical and political concern. So it's no surprise that we bring new questions to the text that early generations did not think to ask. As Hayward notes, this is largely due to our prosperity. Few Westerners now live the life of subsistence farmers. Living in relative prosperity, modern people have come to value a clean environment as a good in itself, as well as part of our own well-being. Contrary to stereotype, the more advanced industrialized nations not only make the environment a priority, they also have a less negative impact on the environment than developing nations in the early stages of industrialization. These facts suggest that good economic policy that leads to prosperity is, in the long run, also good environmental policy.

DISCERNMENT

Jews and Christians agree with environmentalists that we should care for our natural environment. Unfortunately, the environmental movement is diverse, and includes some ideas that contradict the biblical worldview. For instance, pantheism and nature worship are not uncommon in environmental circles. And many environmentalists have an unbiblical view of human beings. Some reduce man to a mere animal who is not different, in kind, from the chimp in the jungle. Others depict human beings not as creative image bearers of God, but as mere consumers of resources, like locusts that move from site to site, consuming everything in their path.

A few years ago, one prominent scientist and environmentalist wrote to me about a subject of mutual interest. The letter was generally cordial, but toward the end, it took a dark turn. This scientist said he disagreed with me that humans were meant to be here. He went on:

> Still, adding over seventy million new humans to the planet each year, the future looks pretty bleak to me. Surely, the Black Death was one of the best things that ever happened to Europe: elevating the worth of human labor, reducing environmental degradation, and, rather promptly, producing the Renaissance. From where I sit, Planet Earth could use another major human pandemic, and pronto!

Not all environmentalists would agree, of course, but this anti-human sentiment is not quite a fringe opinion.

Many Christians interested in environmental stewardship are aware of these problems in the wider movement. They are also aware that many conservative religious believers may care about the environment but oppose "environmentalism," which they identify with apocalyptic scare-tactics in service of political power.

So, to avoid the taint of pantheism, misanthropy, and left-wing politics, many Christian environmentalists now speak of "creation care." This is a rhetorical improvement, since it is explicitly theological. The Bible, after all, speaks of creation rather than of "nature" or the "environment." Still, creation care, if it is to be more than an appealing phrase, must do more than baptize conventional environmental opinion. Believers interested in creation care must exercise the spiritual and intellectual virtue of discernment, because, in the environmental debate, the "chaff" of bad science and anti-human ideology grows up closely beside the "wheat" of good intentions and environmental facts. We cannot just take the "science" for granted, and we should not mistake good intentions for sound environmental policies.

We have to be willing to study and to think hard about a variety of issues related not just to the Bible or theology, but also to climate science and economics. As Hayward argues, environmental policies inevitably involve tradeoffs, so that our moral choice is seldom as easy as choosing "for" or "against" the environment. In some cases, it may be better to recycle paper, but in other circumstances, the environmental impact and energy cost of recycling paper may be higher than simply disposing of it. And many well-meaning environmental regulations often do more damage than the problem they are intended to solve. Subsidies for ethanol, for instance, increase the price of food, reallocate farmland from food to fuel production, and have little if any environmental benefit.

If we are going to be morally serious, and not merely provide religious cover for an irreligious ideology or attempts to increase the power of the state, then believers must take account of such details.

Take, for example, global warming, or "climate change," which in recent years has cast far more heat than light. To be discerning on this issue, we have to ask and answer several different questions. And it's only after answering these questions that we can determine what, if anything, we ought to do about global warming. The first question is a question of fact: Is the earth in a warming trend? We should be able to answer that question, with some degree of certainty, by looking at the scientific evidence. But even if we have evidence that the earth is in a warming trend, it won't tell us whether human activity (like carbon dioxide emissions) is the main cause of that warming. The second question, then, is about cause, and determining cause is much more difficult, and controversial, than determining effect. Pictures of retreating glaciers in Alaska from one decade to the next may be evidence of warming, but they don't tell us why the earth has warmed.

Of course, even if humans are causing the earth to warm, we still need to ask whether this warming, on balance, is bad. This question rarely occurs to those who get their information from the cover of *Newsweek*, but some warming might be good. It might lead to droughts in some places, but to a warmer, wetter, more productive climate elsewhere. The total might be a net gain. Such analysis is complicated and subject to all sorts of uncertainty, but it is essential if we are to know whether the costs of warming outweigh the benefits.

Finally, we come to the public policy question. For even if we are causing catastrophic global warming, we still have to determine what policy, if any, would be likely to make a positive difference. The moral issues surrounding environmental stewardship are not as simple as concluding that, since we must be good stewards, we must have a federally-imposed carbon tax, or carbon-trading scheme, or subsidies for ethanol, or green jobs.

A GOOD PLACE TO START

There are now many religious voices speaking to environmental issues and, unfortunately, not all agree. Even among those who share the same general theological outlook, there is widespread disagreement on the details. If you do not have the time and opportunity to study the issues in depth, this diversity of opinion can be bewildering. It is especially troubling if you find yourself in the position of teaching, preaching, or leading a flock of believers.

In response to this contradictory cacophony, some say that religious leaders should stick to saving souls and avoid public policy debates altogether. This is a perennial temptation. But religious faith, at least in the Judeo-Christian tradition, bears on all of creation, not just on individual souls. To be sure, we have to avoid unintentionally treating theology and Scripture as a wax nose, crimped and twisted to fit a predetermined political agenda. Putting politics before theology is always a risk, whether you're on the left or the right. Still, faith has ethical consequences, so it will inevitably have public consequences as well.

Am I saying that the discerning religious leader should distill the central principles of the biblical perspective, distinguish the signal from the noise in an increasingly fractious public debate, take account of subtle economic and scientific facts, and then carefully apply all of that to specific environmental questions? Well, yes, I suppose I am. It's a tall order, but the circumstances demand it.

Happily, we do not have to do this on our own. There are a few reliable guides, one of whom is Steven F. Hayward. For years, Hayward has studied and written on environmental issues, and is especially keen in analyzing how economics and public policies affect the environment. In the following pages, Hayward covers many of the key elements related to environmental stewardship clearly and dispassionately. And he does so while seeking the biblical wisdom on these questions. His expertise in several disciplines, including politics, economics, and the environment, gives him fresh insights into the biblical text that have eluded many commentators. And, like the biblical texts, Hayward never loses sight of the importance of human beings.

Too often, environmentalists have treated human beings as the problem, rather than as the source of potential solutions. Standing athwart this trend, Hayward joins the company of the late economist Julian Simon, who referred to the creative imagination of human beings as the "ultimate resource," and Pope John Paul II, who argued that "besides the earth, man's principal resource is man himself." In our contemporary debate over the environment, perhaps no insight is more frequently forgotten. In the biblical perspective on humans and the natural world, however, no insight is more important.

INTRODUCTION.
"WHAT WOULD JESUS DRIVE?"

"What Would Jesus Drive?"

This popular bumper-sticker inquiry is merely the most succinct expression of a growing interest in environmental issues among evangelical Christians. Beyond catchy bumper strips are a range of recently founded faith organizations with an environmental focus, such as the Evangelical Environmental Network and its magazine *Creation Care*, the National Religious Partnership for the Environment, the Evangelical Climate Initiative, the Regeneration Project, and the Cornwall Alliance for the Stewardship of Creation.[1] The prominence of the issue of climate change is the most visible aspect of environmental concern today, but there are broader issues at stake involving the uniquely Christian perspective that views nature through the biblical lens of God's creation.

The purpose of this essay is to outline a distinctive Christian perspective on the environment and provide a framework for

Christians to engage environmental issues and environmental activists who approach the subject from a conventional secular viewpoint. There are some important differences between Christian and secular perspectives on the environment. Christian environmentalism will be sometimes opposed to, sometimes parallel to, and sometimes harmonious with conventional secular environmentalism. Understanding the sources of these tensions and harmonies is crucial. There are many temptations and confusions to be avoided; there are many principles of action to embrace and celebrate. Christians who confront environmental issues can make a significant contribution to progress in solving ecological problems. Above all, this essay is intended as a starting point. It does not try to answer all questions or settle the most important questions definitely. Rather it aims to stimulate further thought about humans, our place in the natural world, and the glorification of God's creation.

A deeper understanding of the subject should begin with a brief look at how the issue of the environment fits within the history of Christian social activism, and with reflection on the Christian understanding of humans and the natural world as it emerges from the Bible.

CHAPTER I.
THE ENVIRONMENT IN THE CONTEXT
OF CHRISTIAN SOCIAL ACTION

———————————

Recent Christian interest in the environment is another instance of the crossroads of faith and politics, and as such it is useful to place the issue in long-term context.[2] Christian faith has always been closely involved with current political and social issues, despite the apolitical teaching of the Gospel. In part, this represents working out in real time the implications of Christ's enigmatic counsel to "render unto Caesar what is Caesar's, and render unto God what is God's." In part, it also represents the recognition of social conditions that are an impediment to fulfilling Christian faith, and hence the imperative to work to change those conditions—a proper expression of "works" to manifest our faith, as the Apostle James counsels.[3] Thus, Christian faith can be seen to have played prominent roles in the American Revolution, in the Abolitionist movement, the Temperance movement, and the Civil Rights movement, to name only four American examples. A generation ago, the threat of catastrophic nuclear war preoccupied the attention of many leading

Christian thinkers and activists; although the threat of nuclear catastrophe has not fully receded, the issue gets much less attention today. So it is not surprising or unusual that Christians would turn their attention to environmental issues.

But Christian concern for a current issue does not automatically suggest a clear answer or answers to the problems set forth, reminding us that Christians need to apply the virtue of humility when thinking through what to do. Individual Christians and different denominations have not always been on the right side of some issues, or have been badly divided about what policy conforms to Christian teaching. Rule by the divine right of kings, which today appears as peculiar as leechcraft in medicine, was once accepted as a political postulate of Christianity. But within a century—the blink of an eye in the time-scale of the Christian church—new ideas of democracy and individual rights swept away this old foundation of political legitimacy, with Christian political thinkers in the lead. Both ideas could not be correct, even "for their time." More recent examples should also engage our humility. Even as Christian faith played a central role in the movement for the abolition of slavery both in the British Empire and in the United States in the nineteenth century, there were still many Christian voices that defended the "peculiar institution" as being compatible with, or approved by, Biblical Christianity. Both sides cited the ambiguous Pauline Epistle to Philemon, where Paul pleads the case for forgiveness of the escaped Christian slave Onesimus, in support of their opinions. Both could not have been correct as a matter of moral principle, as Lincoln memorably reminded us in his second inaugural address, noting that both sides—North and South—read the same Bible and prayed to the same God.

Today, Christians are divided over issues central to what is called the "Culture War," such as abortion, gay marriage, and the status of women in the church. Some denominations are literally breaking apart over these issues. There is a fine line between applying biblical faith to social conditions in the service of God's purposes, and becoming an adjunct of current secular political and social trends. A spirit of *discernment* is the most needful thing when considering the intersection of Christian faith and social issues, lest Christian thought become reinterpreted and subsumed as a mere component of contemporary social idealism. Indeed, the allure of compelling secular perspectives on social issues, usually and confusingly derived from the Christian heritage of Western civilization, needs to be regarded as a classic form of temptation.[4] Often there will be overlapping aspects of Christian and secular approaches to social issues. The primary task of a Christian thinker, therefore, is to focus on what is *distinctive* about a Christian approach to an issue.

There is a notable irony to the recent environmental interest among Christians. Many young Christians especially find the environment to be a less acrimonious field than the stalemated social issues of the "Culture War" such as abortion and gay marriage, and therefore a potential avenue to building common ground with the wider culture. Yet, nearly every aspect of the wide bundle of issues that compose the broad field of "the environment" is disputed or contestable, from the basic scientific facts (is catastrophic global warming firmly established? How great is the toxic risk from synthetic chemical compounds? What are the actual rates and principle causes of species extinction? What are the best policy approaches to solving environmental problems?) to the social values we apply to environmental issues, especially the basic issue of the relationship between humans and the natural world around us.

As we shall see, the biblical understanding of humans and the natural world differs in fundamental ways from many "mainstream" environmental views. Christianity places humans—made in the image of God and therefore sharing, to some extent, God's creativity—at the center of creation, whereas most secular environmentalists exalt the natural world in such as way as to make humans a subordinate part of nature, and often as only destructive of nature. This does not mean that Christians will or must be at odds with mainstream secular environmentalism, but it does mean that Christian environmentalism will not be uniform in its application.

CHAPTER II.
ENVIRONMENTALISM TODAY:
MODERN FORMS, ANCIENT ROOTS

———————————

Environmentalism is accurately thought of as a modern phenomenon, yet as with the case of modern concepts of human
rights, Christians will note clear antecedents to modern environmental sentiment in the Bible, especially the account of creation
in Genesis. Indeed, the creation story, the account of the Fall of
Man, the Flood and Noah's Ark all evoke sentiments that would
sound familiar to contemporary environmentalists. Adam's
original sin can also be seen as Man's first act of pollution or
defilement of nature—a display of ingratitude or indifference
to God's bountiful creation. The perfection and abundance of
Man's original condition in Eden, and the corruption of that
state from the Fall, is suggestive of many strains of modern environmentalism that posit a state of harmony between humans and
nature disrupted or corrupted by humans' self-destructive mate-
rialism. Just as Marxism can be understood as a Christian heresy,
this strain of modern environmentalism can be seen as a secular
version of the Fall of Man, with modern environmentalists as

prophets seeking to reverse the Mosaic procession, promising to lead mankind back into the wilderness, eventually redeeming the wilderness in such a manner as to re-establish the Garden of Eden on Earth.

Here one can begin to see problematic aspects of conventional environmentalism from a Christian point of view. Before proceeding, however, it is necessary to offer some definitions so as to clear away a source of confusion. It is common, especially in the media and within the environmental community itself, to speak of "environmentalism" or "the environmental movement" as though it is a narrowly defined or singular category of thought. Even in this introduction to the subject, we have used the term "conventional environmentalism" in this sweeping manner. To be sure, environmental activism, especially among the prominent organizations involved in political battles in Washington, appears very cohesive and monolithic, and the nature of interest-group coalition politics often leads environmental organizations to intransigent positions. But just as there are a large number of Christian denominations, and significant differences of doctrine and theology among Christian denominations, so too there is a wider spectrum of environmental thought within what might stylistically be called the "Green Church." Different kinds of environmentalism should be similarly distinguished. To extend the comparison between the church and environmentalism, one thing unites disparate Christian denominations—the divinity of Jesus Christ. Are there central tendencies of environmentalism? Let us see.

CHAPTER III.

DIFFERENT SHADES OF GREEN: FROM EXTREME UTOPIANISM TO PRACTICAL INCREMENTALISM

It is important to begin with an inventory to separate central tendencies from extreme variations. On the surface, environmentalism is most often regarded as a liberal political cause, though there is no essential reason why this should be so. Indeed, if the proverbial Man from Mars were to drop onto the American scene, nothing would seem more natural than to assume that environmentalism would be a conservative enthusiasm. Among other obvious things, *conservative* and *conservatism* share the same etymological root with conservation and conservationism, and while *conservationism* and *environmentalism* may not be identical, they are clearly blood relatives. The chief reason political conservatives today are estranged from environmentalism has much to do with conservative dislike of the centralized bureaucratic regulation of most environmental laws today. (More about this important point in due course.)

Many conservatives are also put off by the apocalyptic rhetoric that often dominates popular environmental thought. On the other hand, consider the following statement from a prominent political figure: "[There is an] absolute necessity of waging all-out war against the debauching of the environment...The bulldozer mentality of the past is a luxury we can no longer afford. Our roads and other public projects must be planned to prevent the destruction of scenic resources and to avoid need-lessly upsetting the ecological balance."[5] While this sounds like something Al Gore or Ralph Nader would say, in fact it was Ronald Reagan, when he was governor of California, at a time when he was signing into law a series of sweeping new environmental statutes.

Middle-class Americans exhibit environmental sympathy for the most commonsensical of reasons: No one wants to breathe dirty air, drink contaminated water, or eat poisoned food. In some respects, modern environmentalism is an extension of the public health movement, and in fact the Environmental Protection Agency (EPA) can be thought of as a public health bureaucracy writ large. (Most EPA regulations, in fact, are organized around assessments of the effects of pollution on human health and are seldom crafted for conservation pur-poses. And statute-driven government regulatory approaches are incremental rather than transformative.)

All people likewise enjoy unspoiled natural wonders, such as clean beaches, clear rivers and streams, and verdant forests. The establishment of national parks to preserve natural wonders such as Yellowstone and Yosemite for all time is sometimes identified as the beginning of modern conservationism, but in recent years we see monument designations and other forms of permanent preservation extended to areas with less jaw-dropping beauty but equal ecological importance, such as prairie grasslands and desertscapes. This common-sense or practical environmentalism is the basis for the political popularity of environmentalism, and it is not unusual to see environmentally themed bumper stickers on sport-utility vehicles and large RVs. Then, too, the important role of hunters and fishers in supporting conservation and preservation measures belies the stereotype of environmentalists as tree-hugging vegan hippies clad in hemp clothing.

There are more extreme forms of environmentalism that go by such terms as "deep ecology" or are associated with professedly radical groups such as Earth First! or the Earth Liberation Front and their adjuncts in the so-called animal rights movement. These forms of environmentalism, which might be called the "fundamentalist" greens, often exhibit a deep hostility toward humans or human civilization and can be considered a species of revolutionary utopianism. Perhaps the bluntest recent statement of this position was the manifesto of the "Unabomber" of the 1990s, who deplored the whole of what he called "industrial civilization." As recently as January 2010, a book appeared in Britain entitled *Time's Up*, arguing that modern industrial civilization should be dismantled and cities razed to the ground immediately.

For all the radicalism, frequently silly statements, occasional acts of violence, or self-loathing of humanity that often comes from extremists, the central premise—that humans are alienated from nature or that industrial civilization's exploitation of natural resources is self-destructive of both humans and nature—should not be dismissed out of hand. At the heart of extreme environmentalism is a serious challenge: Our environmental problems are not simple matters of weighing tradeoffs between resource use and pollution versus human material wants; in fact, the environment is fundamentally a *philosophical* or spiritual problem, concerning basic questions of human nature itself and humankind's relationship to the natural world. Indeed, the Evangelical Environmental Network's statement of Creation Care takes note of this point: "Many concerned people, convinced that environmental problems are more spiritual than technological, are exploring the world's ideologies and religions in search of non-Christian spiritual resources for the healing of the earth."

While the spiritual and philosophical dimensions of environmental issues are worthy of thoughtful consideration, the radical critiques of "deep ecology" often find expression in mainstream environmentalism in a way that denies or negates the creativity of the human species—the creativity that is one of the essential attributes of humankind's partaking of the image of God. Two younger "next generation" environmentalists, Ted Nordhaus and Michael Shellenberger of the Breakthrough Institute in Oakland, California, have taken note of the implicit misanthropy of conventional environmentalism in a provocative way, writing in their book Break Through: From the Death of Environmentalism to the Politics of Possibility: "[T]he concept of nature in the theological, singular, and exterior way that environmentalists use it can only really be defined as 'that which is not human,' or, in the case of places environmentalists try to preserve, 'that which has not been sullied by humankind.'"6 Environmentalists, Nordhaus and Shellenberger add, "see in housing development only the loss of nonhuman habitat—not the construction of vital human habitat. Thus, the vast majority of environmental strategies aim to constrain rather than unleash human activity."7 Although prudent limits to many human activities are necessary (such as halting overfishing in depleted fisheries), as a general attitude, the "limits to growth" mentality is ultimately self-defeating, as is any social constraint that is contrary to human nature.

CHAPTER IV.
HUMAN ALIENATION FROM NATURE:
A VARIATION OF SIN?

———————

The view that the human species is alienated from nature is, in some respects, a secular version of the idea of original sin, with technology serving as the instrument of temptation. It finds serious consideration from prominent modern thinkers and philosophers, from Edmund Burke on the right to Martin Heidegger on the left. Edmund Burke, the great eighteenth-century Christian, philosopher, and founding thinker of modern conservatism, wrote in his book *A Vindication of Natural Society*: "It is an incontestable truth, that there is more havoc made in one year by Men, of Men, than has been made by all the lions, tigers, panthers, leopards, hyenas, rhinoceroses, elephants, bears, and wolves, upon their several species, since the beginning of the world."[8]

The Romantic movement in the nineteenth century and the Existentialist movement in the twentieth century gradually developed the sophisticated view that technology separates humankind from nature in a fundamental way, and is the cause of our "alienation." It is important to understand that it is not our practical gadgets, such as steam engines and computers, that cause this alienation, but the "technological" way of treating the natural world as an object apart from humanity to be manipulated by humanity, in the manner by which a chemist turns basic compounds into plastic. The point is, according to this view, that the "technological way of thinking" about nature has corrupted human consciousness from the earliest days of human civilization. This view finds its most powerful and complicated expression in modern times in the philosophy of the German existentialist Martin Heidegger, but also in some Christian social thinkers, such as Jacques Ellul.

Like extreme views in many areas of public life, this deeper philosophical current has a way of bleeding over into popular consciousness. Former Vice President Al Gore's book *Earth in the Balance* embraces the view that our environmental problems are a sign of "dysfunctional civilization" and a "deep philosophical crisis in the West." Gore writes: "We seem increasingly eager to lose ourselves in the forms of culture, society, technology, the media, and the rituals of production and consumption, but the price we pay is a loss of our spiritual lives...Our seemingly compulsive need to control the natural world...has driven us to the edge of disaster, for we have become so successful at controlling nature that we have lost our connection to it."[9] In other words, our environmental problems are not just moral in nature, but deeply metaphysical.[10]

Any time a matter is presented as a philosophical problem involving humans, nature, and alienation, the intersection of, and potential conflict with, Christian viewpoints is inevitable. The conflict becomes even more apparent and serious when one notes the frequency with which environmentalism adopts religious language and imagery, sometimes explicitly derived from the Christian tradition, yet emptied of any Christian content. Great natural places, such as the Alaska National Wildlife Refuge, are referred to as "cathedrals" and often are literally suggested as places of worship—not of God, but of nature as a substitute god. Certain self-denying expressions or lifestyle practices of environmentalists resemble nothing so much as the self-denying asceticism of monastic orders of the church. The environmental narratives of return to an uncorrupted state of nature parallel redemption narratives of Christianity; indeed, some environmentalists think of themselves literally as biblical-style prophets or as a new Chosen People who, in a reversal of Moses, promise to lead us back into the Wilderness—perhaps even restoring the Garden of Eden or the Edenlike harmony of a world without sin. Other religious or quasi-religious expressions of environmental sentiment derive from pantheistic or pagan sources. The late environmental pioneer David Brower, for example, came to be known as the "archdruid" of modern environmentalism. One of the confusing ironies of modern environmentalism is that it often manages to be both puritan and pagan at the same time.

There are purely secular forms of environmentalism that nonetheless have a philosophical anthropology that is inimical to a biblical understanding of the issue. Sometimes humans are described as a plague on the planet, apart or separate or alien from the natural world rather than a part of it. Occasionally this self-loathing extends as far as hoping for humankind's extinction, either from deliberate suicide or from a plague represented as the retribution of the rest of nature against humans. For example, a research biologist for the National Park Service named David Graber wrote in the *Los Angeles Times*:

> Human happiness, and certainly human fecundity, are not as important as a wild and healthy planet. I know social scientists who remind me that people are part of nature, but it isn't true. Somewhere along the line—at about a billion years ago, maybe half that— we quit the contract and became a cancer. We have become a plague upon ourselves and upon the Earth. It is cosmically unlikely that the developed world will choose to end its orgy of fossil-energy consumption, and the Third World its suicidal consumption of landscape. Until such time as Homo sapiens should decide to rejoin nature, some of us can only hope for the right virus to come along.[11]

There is also the "Voluntary Human Extinction Movement," whose motto is "May we live long and die out," arguing that

"Phasing out the human race by voluntarily ceasing to breed will allow Earth's biosphere to return to good health."[12]

On the surface, it might not seem that these differences are important to practical policy questions such as how to organize and manage a community recycling program or how to address global warming at the international level, and perhaps these extreme expressions, usually intended to draw attention to unrepresentative points of view, should be ignored. But even in more "mainstream" points of view, there are important differences of understanding and perception of humans and nature that need to be kept in mind and have implications for how environmental problems are treated.

CHAPTER V.
BEGIN AT THE BEGINNING:
HUMANS AND NATURE IN CREATION

A biblical perspective on the environment will differ from secular points of view not merely because of the Lordship of Jesus Christ and the sovereignty of God, but because the Judeo-Christian perspective is fundamentally at odds with these approaches on several key points. In complicated inquiries, it is often best to begin at the beginning, and Christians have a special advantage on this subject because the explicit teaching about the beginning of humans and their relationship to nature is spelled out in categorical terms in the Book of Genesis.

There are at least four distinctive points to be derived from the opening chapters of Genesis:

- The distinctiveness of humans among all the species in nature;
- God's grant of dominion over nature to humans;

- The responsibility for the proper stewardship of nature;
- Sin, which will complicate the foregoing three aspects of humanity's place in the world.

The beginning of Genesis makes clear, first, that the human species is a part of nature, but that humans, being created in the image of God, hold an exalted place in the hierarchy of nature—below the angels but above the mute beasts of the field. This is a crucial point, as many forms of modern environmentalism either portray humans as simply another, equal part of nature (this is the premise of the animal rights movement, for example), or as a grotesque predator against the rest of the order of nature. A human, as C.S. Lewis (among others) pointed out, is the only member of earthly creation with "a new kind of consciousness which could say 'I' or 'me,' which could look upon itself as an object, which knew God, which could make judgments of truth, beauty, and goodness, and which was so far above time that it could perceive time flowing past."[13]

CHAPTER VI.
CONTESTED QUESTIONS ABOUT THE HIERARCHY OF CREATION: FOUR IMPLICATIONS

The hierarchy of humans in the natural order of the universe has several important implications, many of them controversial. First, it helps us remember that "nature" is a term of distinction, rather than a general term for "the totality of all phenomena" as the term is commonly used today. The most basic natural distinction in Genesis is between humans and God, then between man and woman, then between humans and the beasts that move, and then between humans and organic life (plants and trees) that do not enjoy locomotion. Often, modern environmentalism regards nature as a more or less undifferentiated whole. This is the explicit understanding of the "Gaia" hypothesis, for example. The Gaia hypothesis holds that all of nature should be thought of as a single, interconnected organism, of which humans are no more special to the whole than a single strand of hair is to the human body. This kind of approach elevates nature over humans, or into its own object of worship. This is not necessarily a new or modern idea; one can recognize a rough parallel in Genesis in the example of the Ancient Egyptians, who worshiped animals and whose dislike of the Israelites was partly generated by the fact that Israelites were shepherds who ruled over sheep and goats.

Second, humans are bestowed the privilege and responsibility of ruling over the rest of nature: "Then God said, 'Let us make man in our image, according to our likeness; and let them rule over the fish of the sea and over the birds of the sky and over the cattle and over all the earth, and over every creeping thing that creeps on the earth'" (Gen. 1:26). God repeats and amplifies this point with his special blessing for man and woman in the special blessing He offers in the immediate sequel:

> And God blessed them; and God said to them: "Be fruitful and multiply, and fill the earth and subdue it; and rule over the fish of the sea and over the birds of the sky, and over every living thing that moves on the earth." Then God said, "Behold, I have given you every plant yielding seed that is on the surface of the earth, and every tree which has fruit yielding seed; it shall be food for you; and to every beast of the earth and to every bird of the sky and to every thing that moves on the earth which has life, I have given every green plant for food," and it was so. (Gen. 1:28–30)

These passages form the basis of humanity's *dominion* over nature; Genesis makes clear that the provision of nature is

intended for mankind's beneficial use. There is one other important corollary to be observed from the Ten Commandments in
the twentieth chapter of Exodus: The Tenth Commandment
explicitly recognizes the right of mankind to *ownership* of nature,
that is, property rights. ("You shall not covet your neighbor's
house; you shall not covet your neighbor's wife or his male servant or his female servant or his ox or his donkey or anything
that belongs to your neighbor" [Exod. 20:17].) This will be an
important point later on when the economics of environmental
protection is considered.

Third, with rule and privilege comes responsibility. Humanity's
dominion over nature is not the same thing as humanity's *conquest* of nature. Genesis makes this clear in the second chapter, where "the Lord God took the man and put him into the
Garden of Eden to *cultivate and keep it*" (Gen. 2:15, emphasis
added). Although the creation story up to this point emphasizes
the abundant provision of humanity's earthly material needs,
the phrase "to cultivate and keep it" strongly implies that the
paradise of creation does not mean effortless luxury or abundance without limit. Hence the origin of the idea of *stewardship*—the responsibility of humans for the integrity of nature.

Fourth, the character of humanity's dominion and stewardship of
nature changes dramatically with the expulsion of humans from
Eden following Adam's original sin. As previously mentioned,
humanity's ingratitude or carelessness toward God's bounty
can be considered our first act of pollution or environmental

degradation. God's punishment for Adam's sin places humans in a new situation, from a world of abundance to a world of scarcity, requiring supreme toil to survive, as God explains:

> Cursed is the ground because of you;
> In toil you shall eat of it
> All the days of your life.
> Both thorns and thistles it shall grow for you;
> And you shall eat the plants of the field;
> By the sweat of your face
> You shall eat bread,
> Till you return to the ground,
> Because from it you were taken;
> For you are dust,
> And to dust you shall return. (Gen. 3:17–19)

From that moment, until very recently in human history, our existence as "tillers of the soil" has meant a life of struggle with nature for survival itself and for modest progress in material conditions. The natural world around us—and especially the "wilderness"—was primarily regarded not as a source of wonder and beauty but as an inhospitable space to be subdued, conquered, or avoided. This is why the "*untamed* wilderness" was a commonplace phrase. Indeed, the Puritans who came early to American shores in the seventeenth century conceived of their "errand into the wilderness" in terms of vindicating their faith amidst the "adversity" of harsh conditions, similar to Moses and the Israelites in their exodus from Egypt.

Of course, Genesis—like the Old Testament in general—does not use the term "nature" in discussing what we mean when we use it today; the Bible refers to creation. For Christians, the most fundamental distinction is not the distinction between humans and God, but between nature and *supernature*—i.e., the omnipotence of God. Christians will revere the things of the natural world ultimately because of their connection with, and glorification of, their Creator, while secular environmentalists reverse this or even worship nature solely for its own sake.

CHAPTER VII.
THE STORY OF THE FLOOD:
ENVIRONMENTAL CATASTROPHE OR VALIDATION
OF AN ANTHROPOCENTRIC CREATION?

The unknowability of the *supernatural* by rational human reason or the five senses does not diminish its theological intelligibility from scriptural revelation, though this will always be a point of friction between Christian and secular environmentalists. That nature—creation—is meant to be understood as instrumental to the glorification of God and subordinate to God's transcendent and inscrutable purposes is made most evident by what, to modern eyes, surely ranks as the most environmentally confusing story of the Old Testament: God's destruction of nature in the Flood, combined with His preservation and re-creation of nature through Noah's ark. The Flood story turns out to be crucial to the Christian understanding of creation, because in its absence, the destruction of nature, whether from human acts or natural catastrophe, would seem to be evidence against the goodness of God, like other forms of suffering that have always been a pillar of doubt. Theologians have explained

God's tolerance for suffering as a necessary consequence of human free will.

The decadence and evil of humans following the Fall in chapter 3 of Genesis leads God to the surprising repentance of His own creation and the shocking decision to destroy virtually the whole of creation through the Flood:

> Then the Lord saw that the wickedness of man was great upon the earth, and that every intent of the thoughts of his heart was only evil continually. And the Lord was sorry that He had made man on the earth, and He was grieved in His heart. And the Lord said, "I will blot out man whom I have created from the face of the land, from man to animals to creeping things and to the birds of the sky; for I am sorry that I have made them." (Gen. 6:5–7)

This remarkable passage makes clear that God regards humans and nature as an interconnected whole, rather than as separate or different spheres, and that humanity's sins extend to animals, which are not endowed with independent moral judgment and which should otherwise be considered innocent of humanity's sinful rebellion against God. In the first book of Genesis, God looked upon creation and declared it to be "very good," but the onset of human sin corrupted the whole of it: "Now the earth was corrupt in the sight of God" (Gen. 6:11). And so animals and the rest of the natural world pay the price of the Flood along with humans. As God explains to Noah: "I am bringing the flood of water upon the earth, to destroy all flesh in which is the breath of life, from under heaven; everything that is on the earth shall perish" (Gen. 7:17). This carries an implication that is uncomfortable to modern secular environmental thought, namely, that the worth of nature, in God's eyes, depends upon the worth and character of humans at the apex of God's creation and does not have intrinsic worth by itself. If the natural world beyond humanity had a sacredness of its own, God could have chosen to send a plague that destroyed only humans rather than inundating the whole of creation.

After commanding Noah to preserve every living species of animals and birds "to keep offspring alive on the face of all the earth" (Gen. 7:3), God "blotted out every living thing that was upon the face of the land, from man to animals to creeping things and to birds of the sky...and only Noah was left, together with those that were with him in the ark" (Gen. 7:23). The example of Noah as a preserver of nature and the agent of regenerating life remains vivid in contemporary environmental thought and imagery. In fact, the U.S. government panel that is sometimes convened to deliberate over tradeoffs in the protection of endangered species is referred to as the "God squad." There are other aspects of God's commands to Noah that are more difficult to square with conventional modern sensibilities. As Noah loads the ark with males and females of all species in chapter 7 of Genesis, we see for the first time in the Bible the distinction between "clean" and "unclean" animals. While this distinction is given precise form later in the Mosaic dietary laws, it is not explained here or in the other chapters of the Genesis account of the Flood. Biblical scholars offer a wide range of interpretations of this distinction, but one that is relevant to our subject is the idea that a distinction between clean and unclean parts of nature suggests that a perfect cleansing of life on earth is not contemplated.[14]

Moreover, when Noah emerges from the Ark after the flood-waters recede, one of his first acts is to erect an altar to God, upon which he makes a sacrifice of *every clean animal* (Gen. 8:20). From a modern point of view, this seems peculiar and counterintuitive, since the purpose of the Ark is to provide for the regeneration of life: why sacrifice endangered species, and moreover the "clean" ones? In addition, the Bible does not suggest that God required Noah to make this sacrifice. Yet, the Bible tells us that God "smelled the soothing aroma," and thereafter declared a "new covenant" with humans in which God promised, "I will never again curse the ground on account of man, for the intent of man's heart is evil from his youth, and I will never again destroy every living thing, as I have done" (Gen. 8:20–21). Whereas God stipulated in the first chapters of Genesis that mankind and animals are supposed to be veg-etarian, after the Flood, God said, "Every moving thing that is alive shall be food for you; I give all to you, as I gave the green plant" (Gen. 9:3). Today, we would say that God's finding favor in Noah's sacrifice of clean animals suggests a "right" of humanity to the use of animals so long as it is in the purpose of glorifying God, though the Bible does not speak directly of individual "rights" in the way we think of human rights today.

Nonetheless, the Bible clearly establishes what is often called today an "anthropocentric" view of the relationship between humans and nature, though this is something of a distortion. A clear implication of the creation and Flood stories is that nature was created for a transcendent, holy purpose; secular environmentalism sees nature without such purpose. The creation and Flood stories should also convey a cautionary question for modern humans—is extreme consumption or indifference to nature the equivalent of the decadence of the pre-Flood world that offended God? The charge of stewardship in the Bible would seem to suggest that deliberate or careless environmental degradation is a manifestation of evil and sin, for which the primary remedy is the salvation of souls more than the issuance of another government regulation.

The anthropocentric view of the Bible forms the basis, however, for a critique of Christianity as the source of environmental degradation in modern times. One of the longest-lasting attacks came from historian Lynn White in *Science* magazine in 1967, in a famous article entitled "The Historical Roots of Our Ecologic Crisis." Similar to Martin Heidegger's argument that technology separates humans from nature and causes humans to "objectify" nature, White argued that "as we now recognize, somewhat over a century ago science and technology—hitherto quite separate activities—joined to give mankind powers which, to judge by many ecological effects, are out of control. If so Christianity bears a huge burden of guilt."[15] White condemned what he called "orthodox Christian arrogance toward nature," observing that "the whole concept of the sacred grove is alien to Christianity and to the ethos of the West." White concluded that "since the roots of our trouble are so largely religious, the remedy must also be largely religious, whether we call it that or not."[16]

While White hoped that we might come to emulate Francis of Assisi, thereby preserving at least a fragment of Christian heritage, other writers have explicitly advocated replacing Christianity with pantheism, in which nature replaces the God of the Bible. Sociologist Richard Means built upon White's critique, arguing that the Western view of God's transcendence— God as *supernatural*—was precisely the religious problem we had to overcome. Means recommended Zen Buddhism as the preferred alternative to Christian faith. What is striking about these critiques is not merely their overt hostility to Christianity but also the fact that they suppose a religious re-conception of humanity's relation to nature will suffice to change human nature. Means thinks a conversion to pantheism will "destroy" egotism and selfishness. In other words, such critics believe we can achieve a world without sin.

Aside from the theological and anthropological difficulties of this proposition, it is doubtful that either pantheism or a neo-Franciscan ethic will solve actual environmental problems. To the contrary, this tends to be a reflection of a tendency to regard humanity's modern interactions with nature in apocalyptic terms, and an inability to come to grips with dynamic solutions to environmental problems. To understand this point, it is necessary to confront head on the global phenomenon that is arguably not contemplated in the Bible or any other ancient religion: the Industrial Revolution.

Onondaga County Public Library
Syracuse, New York

CHAPTER VIII.
THE CHALLENGE OF THE MODERN WORLD:
WEALTH, PROGRESS, AND MATERIALISM

The Industrial Revolution that began about two hundred years ago has changed humanity's relation to, and attitudes about, nature completely—and sometimes it has generated new views about God and nature, such as those of the Transcendentalists of the nineteenth century. In the first half of the nineteenth century, Alexis de Tocqueville reflected that in America, civilization ended where the wilderness began; life along the frontier was one of "wretchedness," and the wilderness itself generally "impenetrable." To de Tocqueville, the scattered frontier settlers represented "an ark of civilization in the middle of an ocean of leaves."[17] How different from the Puritans' "errand into the wilderness" of the seventeenth century, or de Tocqueville's rendering of the American frontier, is the Transcendentalist attitude toward the wilderness that quickly emerged along with industry, as best expressed in the Wordsworth poem:

One impulse from a vernal wood
May teach you more of man,
Of moral evil and of good
Than all the sages can.[18]

Perry Miller, the great scholar of American Puritanism, reflects on the implications of the Transcendental view of nature: "From vernal wood (along with Niagara Falls, the Mississippi, and the prairies) [America] could learn...more conveniently than from divine revelation....Not that the nation would formally reject the Bible. On the contrary, it could even more energetically proclaim itself Christian and cherish the churches; but it could derive its inspiration from the mountains, the lakes, the forests. There was nothing mean or niggling about these, nothing utilitarian. Thus, superficial appearances to the contrary, America was not crass, materialistic: it is Nature's nation, possessing a heart that watches and receives."[19]

In practical terms, we can see that in wealthy, industrialized nations, it became no longer necessary for the vast majority of people to be "tillers of the soil," securing a tenuous existence through sweaty labor over "cursed" ground. Indeed, in the United States and Europe, over the last century, the proportion of the population engaged in farming has fallen from over 75 percent to less than 5 percent. The rapid material advance of the last two hundred years has provided more comfortable lives in several meaningful ways: It has led to longer lifespans, the conquest of diseases, and the ability of the human population

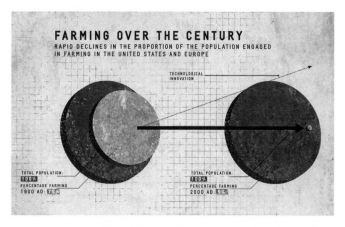

to grow more rapidly and securely than at any time in previous history. (It also has provided the means of transforming social and family relations, liberating women from historically "women's work" on the farm or in the home.) In other words, human ingenuity, technology and innovation have largely succeeded, in wealthy nations at least, in approximating the abundance of the Garden of Eden.

However, no exertion on humanity's part, and no conceivable innovation in technology, can succeed in re-creating the original innocence of humans in the Garden of Eden. There is perhaps a corollary here: This approximation of Eden still partakes fully of human sin. The central insight of environmentalism is that humanity's great leap in material progress has come at a high cost to nature: We tear down entire mountains for their minerals; divert rivers and streams and drain swamps to provide water for modern agriculture and urban use; clear large amounts of forests for other uses, often disrupting crucial habitat for rare animal species; and too often dump our waste byproducts thoughtlessly into the air, water, and land.

This insight contains a paradox, however. Environmentalism arose precisely because we have mitigated the material harshness of human life through the Industrial Revolution; as Aldo Leopold, author of the classic environmental book *A Sand County Almanac*, put it: "These wild things had little human value until mechanization assured us of a good breakfast."[20] It is no coincidence that environmental sensibility arose first and has its strongest influence in wealthy nations. The affluent society does not wish to be the effluent society. Meanwhile, the poorest and most undeveloped nations of Africa, Asia, and Latin America today suffer the worst environmental degradation and have the least public support for environmental protection. It is precisely the wealth and technological innovation (spurred more by markets than by government dictates) of industrialized nations that provides the means for environmental improvement and remediation. Air and water pollution in the United States and Europe, for example, have fallen substantially over the last forty years (and will continue to go down in the coming decades), although they are still worsening in most underdeveloped nations. Forestlands, according to recent United Nations data, are expanding in the United States, Europe, and parts of Asia, but are still contracting in underdeveloped nations.

The point is, our conquest of nature through technology and material progress has enabled our increasing appreciation and concern for it. "The wilderness" is now regarded not as an inhospitable realm to be avoided or conquered, but as a source of wonder to be celebrated and preserved. But this change in outlook extends beyond just our attitudes and sentiments: Prosperity also has become the foundation for environmental improvement.

CHAPTER IX.

THE REVOLUTION IN ENVIRONMENTAL ECONOMICS

At first sight, the connection between rising material standards and environmental improvement seems a paradox, because for a long time, material prosperity and population growth were presumed to be the irreversible engines of environmental destruction. Paul Ehrlich, the famous author of *The Population Bomb*, predicting that runaway population growth would lead to mass starvation and ecological devastation, offered a seemingly scientific formula for this relationship: I = PAT, where I = impact on the planet; P = population, A = affluence, and T = technology. In other words, to minimize our impact on the planet, there need to be fewer humans, we need to be poorer, and we need to have less technology.[21] In the 1970s, the common theme was that the world was in danger of running out of key natural resources, perhaps as soon as the year 2000. The 1972 *Limits to Growth* study, for example, predicted that the world would run out of gold, zinc, mercury, and oil before 1992;[22] the 1980 *Global 2000* report of the U.S. government predicted that the world would face an oil shortage of 20 million barrels a day by 2000 and that oil would cost $100 a barrel. As recently as 1993, David Brower published a full-page ad in the *New York Times* featuring a headline that read, "Economics is a form of brain damage." Not long before, at the 1992 Earth Summit in Rio de Janeiro, environmental activist Hazel Henderson suggested that economists should be sent to re-education camps.[23]

Today, the "population bomb" looks very different from the way it did in 1968, and there has been a revolution in thought about how to regard resource scarcity. Far from experiencing runaway population growth, fertility rates have fallen so fast around the world that the United Nations now forecasts that global population will peak sometime after the middle of the century—within the lifetime of young adults alive today—and then probably begin declining by the end of the century. There are many factors in the decline in fertility rates, but the most powerful correlation appears to be the spread of individual freedom and democracy. Population growth is still the chief driver of serious environmental problems in the developing world, but it no longer appears that the fate of the planet is to experience runaway population growth and mass starvation because of the simple fact that we have been able to expand food production much more quickly than population over the last two generations. Mass famines—once a regular occurrence in the human story—are now seldom experienced, and when they occur, they are chiefly the result of wars or political disruptions, rather than an intrinsic shortage of foodstuffs or basic resource constraints. In the light of this experience, the Evangelical Environmental

Network's Declaration on Creation Care strikes an obsolete note by saying that "these [environmental] degradations are signs that we are pressing against the finite limits God has set for creation. With continued population growth, these degradations will become more severe."[24]

There has been a revolution in environmental economics over the last generation as well, such that almost no environmentalist today would repeat Brower's slogan that "economics is a form of brain damage." To the contrary, one of the most widely accepted ideas in the field today is a concept known as the "Environmental Kuznets Curve" (EKC), named for Nobel laureate Simon Kuznets, who postulated in the 1950s that income inequality first increases and then declines with economic growth as nations develop and grow. Over the last two decades, more and more economists have come to recognize and provide empirical support  for applying Kuznets's concept to the environment. The EKC holds that the relationship between economic growth and environmental quality is an inverted U-shape, according to which environmental conditions deteriorate during early stages of economic growth, but begin to improve after a certain threshold of wealth is achieved. For example, not a single American city falls among the World Bank's ranking of the fifty most polluted cities in the world, and only one European city—Athens—makes the top fifty. It is possible to observe the EKC in action in some developing nations where pollution is now falling after decades of growing worse. Air pollution in Mexico City, for example, has been falling for the last decade, though Mexico City still has a long way to go to match the progress in American cities.

Surveying this new thinking recently, University of California physicist Jack Hollander concluded that "the essential prerequisites for a sustainable environmental future are a global transition from poverty to affluence, coupled with a transition to freedom and democracy."[25] Both the World Bank and the United Nations Environment Program recognize the applicability of the Environmental Kuznets Curve in their latest thinking about sustainable development. The Evangelical Environmental Network's "Declaration on the Care of Creation" gets this point right in its statement that "We recognize that poverty forces people to degrade creation in order to survive; therefore we support the development of just, free economies which empower the poor and create abundance without diminishing creation's bounty."[26]

As mentioned earlier in this book, at the heart of economic development are secure property rights. Just as the role of economic incentives has become more widely appreciated among environmentalists, the key role of property rights—often very insecure in undeveloped, undemocratic nations—is coming into sharper

STEVEN F. HAYWARD

focus as well. Owning parts of nature—whether habitat or actual rare species—sounds counterintuitive to the secular mind (though plainly not to the Old Testament Fathers), but there are more and more case studies demonstrating the effectiveness of property rights approaches to protecting the environment, from ocean fisheries to African and South American forests and even elephants. The role of markets and property rights in promoting environmental protection is conspicuously missing from most evangelical literature about the environment.[27]

A simple thought experiment explains the logic of extending property rights to environmental goods. Suppose our beef cattle industry were organized the same way our ocean fishing tends to operate—a world in which ranchers did not have ranches surrounded by fences, but instead roamed the plains and shot or rounded up as many cows as they wanted. Obviously, we'd run out of cows fairly soon, because the incentives would be wrong; anyone who left a cow behind would be risking that someone else would get to it next. This is a well-known concept referred to as the "tragedy of the commons," arising from the medieval practice in England of allowing anyone to graze as many animals as they wished to on public land. The land quickly became overgrazed. Yet, this is exactly how we manage ocean fisheries—fish are a "common pool" resource in the ocean owned by no one, such that the perverse incentive for every individual fisher is to catch as many fish as possible. A fish left behind is a fish for someone else. This is the chief cause of the collapse of so many ocean fisheries.

47

Some nations—Iceland and New Zealand are the best examples—have effectively preserved and expanded their fisheries through a property rights system known as "catch shares." Essentially, this means designating ownership of territorial waters to individual fishers, who can buy, sell, and trade the rights to catch fish in the area. It is the oceanic equivalent of fencing ranchland for the private ownership and cultivation of cattle and sheep on land. In the United States, Maine's once-threatened lobster industry adopted this approach, and today the lobster beds and the lobster fishing industry are both thriving. Nations that have attempted to manage their fisheries through centralized bureaucratic management have been much less successful. Canada, for example, tried to prevent the collapse of its Atlantic cod fisheries, starting twenty-five years ago with a bureaucratic regulatory program, yet the cod fisheries have continued toward catastrophic collapse.

Examples of the beneficent effects of property rights can be found in other areas of environmental concern, such as endangered species and reforestation—often in less-developed nations. While Africa is still experiencing net deforestation, according to the United Nations' most recent Global Forest Resource Assessment, there is significant reforestation taking place in one African nation—Niger. New studies show that Niger is now greener than it was thirty years ago. "Millions of trees are flourishing," *New York Times* reporter Lydia Polgreen noted; over seven million acres of land have been reforested, "without relying on the large-scale planting of trees and other

48

expensive methods often advocated by African politicians and aid groups for halting desertification."[28]

What explains this turnaround? Polgreen explains the role of property rights:

> Another change was the way trees were regarded by law. From colonial times, all trees in Niger had been regarded as the property of the state, which gave farmers little incentive to protect them. Trees were chopped for firewood or construction without regard to the environmental costs. Government foresters were supposed to make sure the trees were properly managed, but there were not enough of them to police a country nearly twice the size of Texas.
>
> But over time, farmers began to regard the trees in their fields as their property, and in recent years the government has recognized the benefits of that outlook by allowing individuals to own trees. Farmers make money from the trees by selling branches, pods, fruit and bark. Because those sales are more lucrative over time than simply chopping down the trees for firewood, the farmers preserve them.[29]

CHAPTER X.
FOUR KEY LESSONS

Several important lessons emerge from the new thinking about the environment that has emerged over the last generation.

First, do not underestimate the dynamism or resiliency of nature. The default position of many environmentalists to overestimate the severity or intractability of specific environmental problems, often extrapolating current adverse trends to projections of "doom and gloom," has been a cognitive mistake stemming from a too-static view of the world. Both human institutions and ecosystems have shown greater resiliency, capacity for adaptation, and gradual substitution of resource use allowing for significant reversals of adverse trends. Not every environmental problem is a crisis; not every environmental crisis should require the transformation of human nature as a remedy.

Second, we should take seriously the old bumper sticker slogan, "Think Globally, Act Locally." With the exception of climate change and ocean pollution, most environmental issues in the

twenty-first century will be smaller or more specific (plastic bag waste, overuse of antibiotics, and watershed management, to pick just three examples) and more local in scale, and they will require specialized knowledge for their remedy.

Third, policymakers and activists alike need to have a keen sense of *tradeoffs* between competing approaches to solving particular problems. For example, it is not clear that restricting or banning plastic shopping bags will have net environmental benefits, just as research shows that some forms of recycling can result in higher resource waste or the substitution of one kind of waste for another. Paper bags require more energy than plastic bags to manufacture; moreover, recycling some kinds of paper (such as newsprint) requires heavy use of toxic chemicals and generates significant amounts of waste that must be stored in hazardous waste landfills, where space is scarce. Sometimes recycling efforts trade off one environmental waste problem for another. Sorting these out requires careful balancing of fact- and location-specific circumstances. Recycling plastic bags, in some cases, will be more resource-efficient than recycling paper bags. Reusable cloth bags, meanwhile, present still another adverse tradeoff: In humid climates, cloth bags can easily become contaminated with bacteria, presenting a possible source of cross-contamination of groceries. A similar example of difficult tradeoffs can be seen in biofuels, especially corn-based ethanol in the United States. Corn-based ethanol may help reduce overall greenhouse gas emissions (though there is serious controversy about whether this is true) and reduce America's reliance on imported oil, but it requires cultivating more farmland that might otherwise be available for conservation purposes (or to produce food for human consumption), necessitates large amounts of water, and increases water pollution to the Mississippi River basin, aggravating hypoxia (oxygen deprivation, known more popularly as the "dead zone") in the Gulf of Mexico.

Fourth, as the example of ethanol shows, the experience of the last generation should have taught us that most environmental issues are heavily fact-dependent, susceptible to a range of valid and sometimes contradictory assessments, and therefore often fraught with legitimate controversy among specialists. Very often, our facts are woefully incomplete (in the United States, for example, we have no or very poor data on many important aspects of surface water quality), or there is uncertainty about causation. Our technical models of groundwater supplies and conditions, for example, are very deficient. As with any other field of physical science or social science, such as medicine or economics, while vigorous argument and debate are essential, recourse to "values" or sentiment is insufficient to resolve disputes. Just as appeals to "social justice" do little to help find real solutions to the practical problems of poverty, general appeals about environmental disaster or the imperative of "environmental justice" often polarize the issues and detract from progress in finding partial answers.

CHAPTER XI.
SHIFTS IN PUBLIC OPINION

The longstanding environmentalist tendency to predict disaster has been debilitating to the environmental movement. Public opinion surveys in recent years have been detecting rising public skepticism of environmental claims, even as most middle-class people firmly support vigorous environmental protection. *New York Times* columnist Nicholas Kristof, who generally holds conventional environmental views, noted this problem in a column: "The fundamental problem, as I see it, is that environmental groups are too often alarmists. They have an awful track record, so they've lost credibility with the public.... But environmental alarms have been screeching for so long that, like car alarms, they are now just an irritating background noise."[30] It is a fresh application of the old moral fable of the little boy crying "wolf" too often; that is, public weariness with past environmental scares that were overestimated has made it harder to gain traction for the specific and detailed new problems that have arisen.

This appears to be the case with the largest global environmental issue of the moment, climate change, where recent polls show rising public skepticism about the cause and severity. An adequate discussion of climate change is beyond the scope of this essay, but it is an ideal issue to approach through the framework of Christian stewardship and Christian faith. One of the frequent terms heard used in connection with climate change is "uncertainty." In fact the term "uncertain" or "uncertainty" appears 1,300 times in the UN's latest report on the state of scientific knowledge of climate change. MIT atmospheric scientist Kerry Emanuel, who is considered a "mainstream" climate scientist (Vice President Gore has cited Emanuel's work), notes: "To understand long-term climate change, it is essential to appreciate that detailed forecasts cannot, *even in principle*, be made beyond a few weeks. This is because the climate system, at least on short time scales, is *chaotic*" (emphasis in original).[31] Emanuel also cautions: "Scientists are most effective when they provide sound, impartial advice, but their reputation for impartiality is severely compromised by the shocking lack of political diversity among American academics, who suffer from the kind of group-think that develops in cloistered cultures."[32] The discussion of uncertainty in climate change often elicits charges of bad faith against the climate "skeptics" who refer to uncertainty, but as Emanuel suggests, the issue has become dangerously politicized on both sides.

It is useful, though, to set aside the arguments about uncertainty in climate science, and consider uncertainty in policy responses that might be adopted to deal with climate change. Climate change is unlike any other issue the world has ever faced in one important respect: The prospective harms are mostly decades in the future, but significant policy responses would need to be implemented very soon in order to avoid the prospective damages. This is not as clear-cut as it might seem: There is large uncertainty about the effects different policy responses might have on both economic well-being (especially of developing nations) and the effectiveness of greenhouse gas reductions themselves. There are ferocious arguments about policy strategy amongst scientists and policymakers who have little or no disagreement about the underlying science of climate change.

Keeping abreast of even the basics on climate change issues can be a full-time job. What attitude should a person of faith bring to the table? The New Testament virtue of humility is the most needful thing in the climate debate today (and a great many other issues)—not merely about what we think we know and what we ought to do about it, but more generally because the lack of humility, intellectual and otherwise, has made much of the environmental debate poisonous. Indeed, humility is the one genuinely scarce resource that only believing Christians can supply in the needed amount.

Hence, the guidance of the Cornwall Declaration is worth taking to heart:

While some environmental concerns are well founded and serious, others are without foundation or greatly exaggerated. Some well-founded concerns focus on human health problems in the developing world arising from inadequate sanitation, widespread use of primitive biomass fuels like wood and dung, and primitive agricultural, industrial, and commercial practices; distorted resource consumption patterns driven by perverse economic incentives; and improper disposal of nuclear and other hazardous wastes in nations lacking adequate regulatory and legal safeguards.[33]

Whereas the EEN's Creation Care statement reads, "We commit ourselves to work for responsible public policies which embody the principles of biblical stewardship of creation,"[34] the Cornwall Declaration offers an important counterpoint: "Public policies to combat exaggerated risks can dangerously delay or reverse the economic development necessary to improve not only human life but also human stewardship of the environment."[35]

CHAPTER XII.
LIBERTY AND THE ENVIRONMENT:
THE SOBERING PARABLE OF JOSEPH AND
THE ISRAELITES IN EGYPT

The contrasting example of property rights and market-oriented approaches to problems of resource scarcity raises the general problem that conventional environmentalism over-whelmingly favors political, rather than market, solutions to environmental problems, often advocating vast new centralized government power. This is most especially true today in con-nection with climate change, where the leading policy idea is extensive political control of energy resources on a global scale, even though there are numerous alternative policies that might be pursued, such as "geo-engineering."[36]

Here it may be useful to refer once again to Genesis, to a story later in the book that tends to be overlooked in consideration of what Genesis has to say about humans and nature in the early chapters: the story of Joseph and his rise to become Pharaoh's right-hand man, as told in chapters 41 through 47. It provides a parable for the defects of political control over resources. An important caveat should be noted here before proceeding, however. Theologians, ministers, and laypeople generally do not—and should not—read major Bible passages for their political implications, and the unorthodox or idiosyncratic interpretation I am about to offer is not intended to supersede the traditional teachings about Joseph in Egypt that Jewish and Christian scholars have brought to light over the centuries. However, I do think that looking afresh at this story in light of modern concerns about resource management can illuminate some enduring aspects of human experience, demonstrating that for all of the social and material change over the last few millennia, some things remain unchanged.

Most readers concentrate on the relationship of Joseph and his brothers and miss the potential socioeconomic lesson that appears in the part of the story concerning Joseph's interpretation of Pharaoh's dream of the seven fat cows and the seven lean cows, and his dream of the seven plump ears of grain and the seven thin and scorched ears of grain (Gen. 41.) Joseph, brought up from slave quarters to appear before Pharaoh, interprets the paired dream as a prophecy of seven abundant, prosperous years to be followed by seven years of famine. Joseph goes on, uninvited, to give Pharaoh policy advice, namely, that Pharoah should appoint what sounds in today's terms like a "policy czar":

And now let Pharaoh look for a man discerning and wise, and set him over the land of Egypt. Let Pharaoh take action to appoint overseers in charge of the land, and let him exact a fifth of the produce of the land of Egypt in the seven years of abundance. Then let them gather all the food of these good years that are coming, and store up the grain for food in the cities under Pharaoh's authority, and let them guard it. And let the food become as a reserve for the land for the seven years of famine which will occur in the land of Egypt, so that the land may not perish during the famine. (Gen. 41:33–36)

In other words, the government will take command of resources, and have a "wise" person (today we might call such a person a policymaker) ration resources to the people. Small wonder that the next verse reads: "Now the proposal seemed good to Pharaoh and to all his servants." Naturally, the person Pharaoh chose to perform this task was the man who thought of it: Joseph.

Leon Kass, author of a major commentary on the Book of Genesis, observes how convenient this advice is to a ruler looking to expand his power: "The plan Joseph proposes is music to Pharaoh's ears: a prime minister, loyal only to him, backed by an army of bureaucrats, will centralize control over the entire land and its food supply. A silent implication is surely not lost on Pharaoh: during the years of famine, the central administration will use the dispersal of food to further augment and consolidate Pharaoh's power, weakening all possible rivals among the Egyptian nobility and making the people entirely dependent on Pharaoh's rule and deed."[37]

The parallel with modern environmental prophecies of doom requiring vast new political power over people and resources is hard to avoid, as Kass makes evident in the next part of his commentary: "[Pharaoh] is delighted not with the prophecy, but with the plan. Joseph, who evinces the sagacity of the elite and who speaks with godlike assurance, has provided Pharaoh with a defensible and justifiable plan to consolidate his power and to appear as a savior of the people. A divinely sent evil requires drastic measures to avert it...the forecast of disaster will provide the opportunity for Pharaoh to display and acquire more god-like powers."[38]

It is striking how this passage parallels the views of many modern environmental prophets, who advocate for centralized political control of people and resources on a global scale. Back in the 1960s and 1970s, Paul Ehrlich openly argued in favor of "coercion" by governments to lower birthrates (a good deal of which took place in India and other developing nations, where governments forcibly sterilized thousands of men and women), and today argues for a global environmental authority insulated from democratic accountability to "constrain" (Ehrlich's term) resource use. Gus Speth of Yale University, a senior adviser on environmental issues to President Jimmy Carter back in the

1970s, argues in favor of a "world environment organization" modeled after U.S. regulatory agencies where "a small group of officials is writing laws for the country."[39] It is not difficult to envision former Vice President Gore as a modern-day version of Joseph.

The rest of the story of Joseph and the seven years of plenty and seven years of famine is equally instructive, because what appears to start out as reasonable precautions against famine evolves into a sequence of events that ends with the Israelites being cast into four hundred years of slavery under Pharaoh. Joseph starts out by taking all the "surplus" grain and moving it to the cities, thereby making the countryside dependent on the city: "So he gathered all the food of these seven years which occurred in the land of Egypt, and placed the food in the cities; he placed in every city the food from its own surrounding fields" (Gen. 41:48). Kass comments: "We are even invited to wonder whether this excessive gathering and storage of grain—at the expense of saving enough for replanting—might itself have contributed to (not to say caused) the famine in the years that followed."[40] In other words, the policy of Joseph may have helped to cause the very outcome it was intended to avoid. There are certainly many modern examples of this kind of unintended and perverse result of well-meaning policies of resource control.

In the fullness of time, Joseph's command of food resources extends beyond grain. The final aspect of this parable comes in chapter 47, when the starving Israelites, whom the Egyptians had grudgingly allowed to settle with their livestock in the province of Goshen and thus become Egyptian citizens, appeal to Joseph to be rescued. After they have exhausted all their food and their money savings and become wholly dependent on the government, as it were, Joseph says:

> "Give up your livestock, and I will give you food for your livestock, since your money is gone." So they brought their livestock to Joseph, and Joseph gave them food in exchange for their horses and the flocks and the herds and the donkeys. And he fed them with food in exchange for all their livestock that year. (47:16–17)

Having now surrendered themselves into a state of complete dependency, the next year of famine finds the Israelites reduced to offering willingly to enter a state of slavery, since they have nothing left of their own with which to bargain or trade:

> And when that year was ended, they came to him the next years and said to him, "We will not hide from our lord that our money is all spent, and the cattle are my lord's. There is nothing left for my lord except our bodies and our lands. Why should we die before your eyes, and both we and our land? Buy us and our land for food, and we and our land will be slaves to Pharaoh. So give us seed, that we may live and not die, and that the land may not be desolate." So Joseph

bought all the land of Egypt for Pharaoh, for every
Egyptian sold his field, because the famine was severe
upon them. Thus the land became Pharaoh's. And as
for the people, he removed them to the cities from one
end of Egypt's border to the other. Only the land of
the priests did he not buy....Then Joseph said to the
people, "Behold, I have today bought you and your
land for Pharaoh; now here is seed for you, and you
may sow the land. And at the harvest you shall give a
fifth to Pharaoh, and four-fifths shall be your own for
seed of the field and for your food and for those of
your households and as food for your little ones." So
they said, "You have saved our lives! Let us find favor
in the sight of our lord, and *we will be Pharaoh's slaves*."
(47:18–25, emphasis added)

Several observations should be made about this rich passage.
First, this story offers a striking preview of a favorite tactic of
twentieth-century totalitarian regimes, such as Romania and
the Soviet Union, which made it a central practice to move
populations forcibly into cities and out of the countryside, while
closely controlling the remaining private production.

Second, we see an example of another anti-democratic and
unequal practice—the exemption of certain classes of people
from the laws and regulations imposed on the general population, or imposed on specific minorities. In the story of Joseph,
the priests are exempted from having their lands consolidated

and controlled by Pharaoh. This finds its rough equivalent today in the prophets of environmental doom who nonetheless exempt themselves from their recommended frugality for the middle class by continuing to live high-consumption lifestyles (e.g., flying private jets and living in multiple large residences).

Third, note that the tithe of production for Pharaoh shall henceforth be one-fifth—twice the normal one-tenth tithe recommended elsewhere in the Bible. The 10-percent tithe seen repeatedly throughout the Bible should certainly not be read as a literal prescription for tax policy or political economy more generally, but this little detail illustrates the rapacious nature of grasping tyrants with unchecked power.

Above all, the story of Joseph's Egyptian regency points to the peril of how willing dependency on centralized political solutions can lead to the voluntary surrender of individual liberty. To borrow the popular language of environmentalism, real solutions to environmental problems need to be compatible with individual liberty and democracy if they are to be sustainable.

CONCLUSION:
STEPS FOR FURTHER THOUGHT AND ACTION

What should a person of faith take away from these preliminary reflections? There are lots of calls for practical action, such as supporting specific legislation in Washington, or, on a personal level, altering consumption and conservation habits along the lines of various lists of "Fifty Ways to Save the Planet" that typically include tips and recommendations on recycling, energy use, taking shorter showers, and what kinds of foods to eat. Many of these changes in habits are worthy not so much for their aggregate impact, but for the way in which they reinforce conscious stewardship of resources. A simple Internet search will produce many useful lists.

However, the energy use of that Internet search may generate as much carbon dioxide as boiling a kettle of tea—a small amount by itself, to be sure, but when combined with the exploding Internet use overall adds up to a large amount—possibly more than 5 percent of total emissions in the United States according to one controversial estimate. Likewise, compact fluorescent

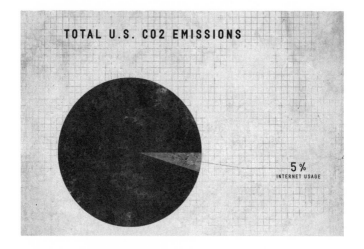

TOTAL U.S. CO2 EMISSIONS

5 %
INTERNET USAGE

light (CFL) bulbs, whose use is recommended on virtually every list of "Fifty Ways to Save the Planet," do indeed use much less electricity, but contain mercury and require disposal in scarce hazardous waste facilities rather than regular trash or recycling programs. As CFL use expands, this problem will need to be solved better than it is today.

This does not mean that consumers should not use CFLs, but it does serve to illustrate a central point of this essay, namely, that tradeoffs and second-order effects are too often left out of account in conversation about the environment. The example of the tradeoffs of CFLs, or of corn-based ethanol mentioned before, illustrate a corollary point, namely, that "the environment" is not an indivisible thing. When we speak

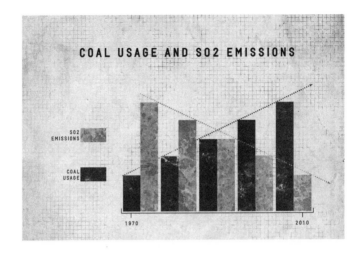

of "the environment," or of "nature" or creation, we are speaking of an immensely complex reality that, like medicine, often requires specialized knowledge of very small parts of the whole. One common impulse of modern times is to seek for systematic, large-scale solutions to social problems. Sometimes large-scale solutions are necessary and appropriate to the environment: National standards for technological performance, such as automobile tailpipe standards that have cut emissions from new autos by 99 percent, have played an important role in improving air quality; similar performance standards for coal-fired power plants have cut sulfur dioxide emissions by 66 percent since 1970. But going forward, many environmental problems will require local knowledge and local action. To extend the comparison with medicine, while there is an important role for general practitioners, most progress comes from specialists.

People of faith motivated by environmental issues can therefore bring two contributions. First, as in other modern fields of endeavor that depend on specialized knowledge, students with a scientific interest should take up earth sciences, engineering, and related disciplines. Many current environmental problems have found their remedies chiefly from technology that scientists and engineers have discovered. In the humanities, there is an equal need for lawyers, economists, historians, and other intellectual pursuits that bear on institutional structure and reform. What will unite many specialized pursuits in this century will be the entrepreneur (in fact, the term "enviro-preneur" is coming into fashion) who finds ways to bring new green technology to the mass marketplace.

Second, Christian faith represents a "speciality" of sorts when it comes to the environment, precisely because of the different perspective on humans and creation that derives from the Christian tradition. Environmental problems can be considered a modern tribulation, through which faithful Christians must pass to enter the Kingdom of God (Acts 14:22), though not necessarily the kind of tribulations associated with the end times in Christian eschatology, which is how many secular environmentalists view our ecological tribulations. Just as Christian faith is a message of hope for humanity, so too is a Christian perspective on the environment a message of hope for creation.

People of faith should bring their own distinctive perspective to bear on the problems facing creation, seeing the redemption of nature beginning with the redemption of our souls, rather than merely becoming an adjunct to the latest fashionable secular trend. C. S. Lewis warned, "The danger of mistaking our merely natural, though legitimate, enthusiasms for holy zeal is always great."[41] Modern environmentalism does not suffer from a lack of zeal. Too often, it suffers the defect of too much zeal and not enough thoughtfulness. The main point of this book is that environmental issues require more serious thought than they often receive in the media or in the hands of activists. Being more thoughtful through the perspective of faith is an important action step in our age—maybe the most important action of all.

ABOUT THE AUTHORS

Steven F. Hayward is the F. K. Weyerhauser Fellow at the American Enterprise Institute. He is the coauthor of the annual *Index of Leading Environmental Indicators*; the producer and host of *An Inconvenient Truth ... or Convenient Fiction?*, a rebuttal to Al Gore's documentary; and the author of many books on environmental topics. He has written biographies of Presidents Jimmy Carter and Ronald Reagan and of Winston Churchill. Mr. Hayward is also a senior fellow at the Pacific Research Institute.

Jay W. Richards is a senior fellow at the Discovery Institute. In recent years, he has been a visiting fellow at the Heritage Foundation and a research fellow and director of Acton Media at the Acton Institute. Mr. Richards has written many academic articles, books, and popular essays on a wide variety of subjects. His most recent book is *Money, Greed, and God: Why Capitalism Is the Solution and Not the Problem* (HarperOne, 2009). He is also executive producer of several documentaries, including *The Call of the Entrepreneur, The Birth of Freedom,* and *Effective Stewardship* (Acton Media and Zondervan, 2009). Mr. Richards has a PhD in philosophy and theology from Princeton Theological Seminary.

ENDNOTES

1. See, especially, the "Evangelical Declaration on the Care of Creation," the founding statement of the Evangelical Environmental Network, http://www.creationcare.org/resources/declaration.php, and the "Cornwall Declaration," an interfaith statement produced by the Acton Institute, http://www.acton.org/ppolicy/environment/cornwall.php. Most major denominations have adopted formal statements about the environment. A listing of major faith-based environmental organizations can be found at: http://www.acton.org/ppolicy/environment/ppolicy_environment_theology_orgs.php.

2. Note that Christian interest in the environment is not strictly a twenty-first-century interest. The Christian apologist and philosopher Francis Schaeffer wrote well on the subject in his 1970 book *Pollution and the Death of Man* (recently re-issued by Crossway Books). Though some specific examples are obviously dated, Schaeffer offered many enduring Christian insights that hold up today, such as: "We treat nature with respect because God made it. When an orthodox, evangelical Christian mistreats or is insensible to nature, *at that point* he is more wrong than the hippie who had no real basis for his feeling for nature and yet sensed that man and nature should have a relationship beyond that of spoiler and spoiled" (77).

3. James 2:20 and 2:24.

4. Cambridge University's Edward Norman offered a valuable warning about this temptation in his 1979 book *Christianity and the World Order* (Oxford University Press): "True religion points to the condition of the inward soul of man. It is therefore skeptical of the contemporary passion of Christians to reinterpret the faith so that it shall become a component of the modern world's political idealism. In Christianity, as it was delivered by the saints and

scholars of the centuries, men are first directed to the imperfections of their own natures, and not to the rationalized imperfections of human society" (76).

5. Ronald Reagan, "Our Environmental Crisis," *Nation's Business*, February 1970, 557–58.

6. Ted Nordhaus and Michael Shellenberger, *Break Through: From the Death of Environmentalist to the Politics of Possibility* (Boston: Houghton-Mifflin, 2007), 94–95.

7. Ibid., 120.

8. Edmund Burke, *A Vindication of Natural Society* (Liberty Fund edition, 1982), 16.

9. Al Gore, *Earth in the Balance: Ecology and the Human Spirit* (Boston: Houghton-Mifflin, 1992), 221, 225.

10. See Steven F. Hayward, "The Fate of the Earth in the Balance," *AEI Energy and Environment Outlook*, October 2006, http://www.aei.org/outlook/25033.

11. David M. Graber, "Mother Nature as a Hothouse Flower," *Los Angeles Times*, October 22, 1989, BR1.

12. See http://www.vhemt.org/.

13. C. S. Lewis, *The Problem of Pain* (London: Centenary Press, 1940), 77.

14. See Thomas L. Pangle, *Political Philosophy and the God of Abraham* (Baltimore: Johns Hopkins University Press), 112–13.

15. Lynn White, "The Historical Roots of Our Ecological Crisis," *Science* 155, no. 3767 (1967): 1203–07. White also seemed to have been skeptical that democracy and ecology are compatible, offering the brief observation: "Our ecologic crisis is the product of an emerging, entirely novel, democratic

culture. This issue is whether a democratized world can survive its own implications. Presumably we cannot unless we rethink our axioms" (1204). White is
not specific as to what these axioms are.

16. White, "The Historical Roots of Our Ecological Crisis," 1206.

17. Alexis de Tocqueville, *Journey to America*, ed. J.P. Mayer, trans. George
Lawrence (London: Faber, 1959), 341.

18. William Wordsworth, "The Tables Turned," (1798), lines 21–24.

19. Perry Miller, *Errand into the Wilderness* (Harvard University Press, 1956),
209.

20. Aldo Leopold, *A Sand County Almanac: And Sketches from Here and There*
(Oxford University Press, 1949), vii.

21. Paul R. Ehrlich and John P. Holdren, "Impact of Population Growth,"
Science 171 (1971): 1212–17.

22. Donella H. Meadows, Dennis L. Meadows, Jorgen Randers, and William
W. Behrens III, *The Limits to Growth* (New York: Universe Books, 1972).

23. See http://reason.com/blog/2008/04/11/is-economics-destroying-
the-wo. *Reason* magazine science editor Ron Bailey reports: "In 1992, at the
first Earth Summit in Brazil, I listened to environmentalist dim bulb, Hazel
Henderson, declare to a crowd of activists that 'economics is brain damage.'
Henderson went on to suggest to the hooting and hollering delight of the
crowd that all economists be rounded up and put into re-education camps."

24. See http://www.creationcare.org/resources/declaration.php.

25. Jack M. Hollander, *The Real Environmental Crisis: Why Poverty, Not Affluence, Is
the Environment's Number One Enemy* (University of California Press, 2003), 3.

26. See http://www.creationcare.org/resources/declaration.php.

27. There are a few notable exceptions, such as Scott Saban of Floresta, a Christian nonprofit organization working on deforestation and poverty issues in the developing world. Writing on the Creation Care blog deepgreenconversation.org, Saban observes: "[E]nvironmentalism is often depicted as being against private property. Yet at Floresta we have found ourselves advocating for property rights. Poor farmers who have the right to use wood and products from trees they plant will be much more likely to plant and care for them in the first place. Similarly poor farmers are more effective stewards of land that they are assured of being able to use in the future" (see http://deepgreenconversation.org/christian-environmentalism/). But this is about the only mention of property rights in the entire Evangelical Environmental Network or Creation Care literature.

28. Lydia Polgreen, "In Niger, Trees and Crops Turn Back the Desert," *New York Times*, February 11, 2007.

29. Ibid.

30. Nicholas D. Kristof, "I Have a Nightmare," *New York Times*, March 12, 2005, available at http://www.nytimes.com/2005/03/12/opinion/12kristof.html.

31. Kerry Emanuel, *What We Know About Climate Change* (Boston: MIT Press, 2007), 31.

32. Emanuel, *What We Know About Climate Change*, 67.

33. See http://www.acton.org/ppolicy/environment/cornwall.php.

34. See http://www.creationcare.org/resources/declaration.php.

35. See http://www.acton.org/ppolicy/environment/cornwall.php.

36. "Geoengineering," or "solar radiation management," refers to a suite of

policy options based on various technical means of deliberately reflecting some portion of solar radiation away from the earth such as to reduce the greenhouse effect. Such ideas range from cloud brightening with artificially generated sea spray (already tested on a small scale), high-altitude sulfate injection (essentially mimicking the cooling effect of volcanic activity), to orbital mirrors. Although controversial, leading scientific organizations in the United States and Europe are actively studying the idea.

37. Leon R. Kass, *The Beginning of Wisdom: Reading Genesis* (University of Chicago Press, 2003), 566.

38. Ibid., 556, 557.

39. See Paul Ehrlich and Anne Ehrlich, *One with Nineveh: Politics, Consumption, and the Human Future* (Washington, D.C.: Island Press, 2002), 288–317; Matthew Connelly, *Fatal Misconception: The Struggle to Control World Population* (Cambridge: Harvard Belknap Press, 2008); Gus Speth, *Red Sky at Dawn* (New Haven: Yale University Press, 2003), 176–77.

40. Kass, *The Beginning of Wisdom*, 567.

41. C. S. Lewis, *God in the Dock: Essays on Theology and Ethics* (Wm. B. Eerdmans Publishing Company, 1994), 198.

NOTES

NOTES

Board of Trustees

Kevin B. Rollins, *Chairman*
Senior Adviser
TPG Capital

Tully M. Friedman, *Treasurer*
Chairman and CEO
Friedman Fleischer & Lowe, LLC

Gordon M. Binder
Managing Director
Coastview Capital, LLC

Arthur C. Brooks
President
American Enterprise Institute

The Honorable
Richard B. Cheney

Harlan Crow
Chairman and CEO
Crow Holdings

Daniel A. D'Aniello
Cofounder and Managing Director
The Carlyle Group

John V. Faraci
Chairman and CEO
International Paper

Christopher B. Galvin
Chairman
Harrison Street Capital, LLC

Raymond V. Gilmartin
Harvard Business School

Harvey Golub
Chairman and CEO, Retired
American Express Company

Robert F. Greenhill
Founder and Chairman
Greenhill & Co., Inc.

Roger Hertog

Bruce Kovner
Chairman
Caxton Associates, LP

Marc S. Lipschultz
Partner
Kohlberg Kravis Roberts & Co.

John A. Luke Jr.
Chairman and CEO
MeadWestvaco Corporation

Robert A. Pritzker
President and CEO
Colson Associates, Inc.

J. Peter Ricketts
President and Director
Platte Institute for Economic
 Research, Inc.

Edward B. Rust Jr.
Chairman and CEO
State Farm Insurance Companies

D. Gideon Searle
Managing Partner
The Serafin Group, LLC

The American Enterprise Institute
for Public Policy Research

Founded in 1943, AEI is a nonpartisan, nonprofit research
and educational organization based in Washington, D.C.
The Institute sponsors research, conducts seminars and
conferences, and publishes books and periodicals.

AEI's research is carried out under three major programs: Economic Policy Studies, Foreign Policy and
Defense Studies, and Social and Political Studies. The
resident scholars and fellows listed in these pages are part
of a network that also includes ninety adjunct scholars at
leading universities throughout the United States and in
several foreign countries.

The views expressed in AEI publications are those of
the authors and do not necessarily reflect the views of
the staff, advisory panels, officers, or trustees.

Mel Sembler
Founder and Chairman
The Sembler Company

Wilson H. Taylor
Chairman Emeritus
CIGNA Corporation

William H. Walton
Managing Member
Rockpoint Group, LLC

William L. Walton
Chairman
Allied Capital Corporation

The Honorable
Marilyn Ware

James Q. Wilson
Boston College and
 Pepperdine University

Emeritus Trustees

Willard C. Butcher

Richard B. Madden

Robert H. Malott

Paul W. McCracken

Paul F. Oreffice

Henry Wendt

Officers

Arthur C. Brooks
President

David Gerson
Executive Vice President

Jason Bertsch
Vice President, Development

Henry Olsen
Vice President; Director,
 National Research Initiative

Danielle Pletka
Vice President, Foreign and Defense
 Policy Studies

Council of Academic
Advisers

James Q. Wilson, *Chairman*
Boston College and
 Pepperdine University

Alan J. Auerbach
Robert D. Burch Professor of
 Economics and Law
University of California, Berkeley

Eliot A. Cohen
Paul H. Nitze Professor of Advanced
 International Studies
Johns Hopkins University

Martin Feldstein
George F. Baker Professor
 of Economics
Harvard University

Robert P. George
McCormick Professor of Jurisprudence
Director, James Madison Program
 in American Ideals and Institutions
Princeton University

Gertrude Himmelfarb
Distinguished Professor of History
 Emeritus
City University of New York

R. Glenn Hubbard
Dean and Russell L. Carson Professor
 of Finance and Economics
Columbia Business School

John L. Palmer
University Professor and Dean
 Emeritus
Maxwell School of Citizenship and
 Public Affairs
Syracuse University

Sam Peltzman
Ralph and Dorothy Keller
 Distinguished Service Professor
 of Economics
Booth School of Business
University of Chicago

George L. Priest
John M. Olin Professor of Law
 and Economics
Yale Law School

Jeremy A. Rabkin
Professor of Law
George Mason University
School of Law

Richard J. Zeckhauser
Frank Plumpton Ramsey Professor
of Political Economy
Kennedy School of Government
Harvard University

Research Staff

Ali Alfoneh
Resident Fellow

Joseph Antos
Wilson H. Taylor Scholar in Health
Care and Retirement Policy

Leon Aron
Resident Fellow; Director,
Russian Studies

Paul S. Atkins
Visiting Scholar

Michael Auslin
Resident Scholar

Claude Barfield
Resident Scholar

Michael Barone
Resident Fellow

Roger Bate
Legatum Fellow in Global Prosperity

Walter Berns
Resident Scholar

Andrew G. Biggs
Resident Scholar

Edward Blum
Visiting Fellow

Dan Blumenthal
Resident Fellow

John R. Bolton
Senior Fellow

Karlyn Bowman
Senior Fellow

Alex Brill
Research Fellow

John E. Calfee
Resident Scholar

Charles W. Calomiris
Visiting Scholar

Lynne V. Cheney
Senior Fellow

Steven J. Davis
Visiting Scholar

Mauro De Lorenzo
Visiting Fellow

Christopher DeMuth
D. C. Searle Senior Fellow

Thomas Donnelly
Resident Fellow

Nicholas Eberstadt
Henry Wendt Scholar in
Political Economy

Jon Entine
Visiting Fellow

John C. Fortier
Research Fellow

Newt Gingrich
Senior Fellow

Jonah Goldberg
Visiting Fellow

Scott Gottlieb, M.D.
Resident Fellow

Kenneth P. Green
Resident Scholar

Michael S. Greve
John G. Searle Scholar

Kevin A. Hassett
Senior Fellow; Director,
Economic Policy Studies

Steven F. Hayward
F. K. Weyerhaeuser Fellow

Robert B. Helms
Resident Scholar

Frederick M. Hess
Resident Scholar; Director,
Education Policy Studies

Ayaan Hirsi Ali
Resident Fellow

R. Glenn Hubbard
Visiting Scholar

Frederick W. Kagan
Resident Scholar; Director,
AEI Critical Threats Project

Leon R. Kass, M.D.
Madden-Jewett Chair

Andrew P. Kelly
Research Fellow

Desmond Lachman
Resident Fellow

Lee Lane
Resident Fellow; Codirector,
AEI Geoengineering Project

Adam Lerrick
Visiting Scholar

Philip I. Levy
Resident Scholar

Lawrence B. Lindsey
Visiting Scholar

John H. Makin
Visiting Scholar

Aparna Mathur
Resident Scholar

Lawrence M. Mead
Visiting Scholar

Allan H. Meltzer
Visiting Scholar

Thomas P. Miller
Resident Fellow

Charles Murray
W. H. Brady Scholar

Roger F. Noriega
Visiting Fellow

Michael Novak
George Frederick Jewett Scholar
in Religion, Philosophy, and
Public Policy

Norman J. Ornstein
Resident Scholar

Richard Perle
Resident Fellow

Mark J. Perry
Visiting Scholar

Tomas J. Philipson
Visiting Scholar

Alex J. Pollock
Resident Fellow

Vincent R. Reinhart
Resident Scholar

Michael Rubin
Resident Scholar

Sally Satel, M.D.
Resident Scholar

Gary J. Schmitt
Resident Scholar; Director,
Advanced Strategic Studies

Mark Schneider
Visiting Scholar

David Schoenbrod
Visiting Scholar

Nick Schulz
DeWitt Wallace Fellow; Editor-in-Chief,
American.com

Roger Scruton
Resident Scholar

Apoorva Shah
Research Fellow

Kent Smetters
Visiting Scholar

Christina Hoff Sommers
Resident Scholar; Director,
W. H. Brady Program

Tim Sullivan
Research Fellow

Phillip Swagel
Visiting Scholar

Marc Thiessen
Visiting Fellow

Bill Thomas
Visiting Fellow

Alan D. Viard
Resident Scholar

Peter J. Wallison
Arthur F. Burns Fellow in
Financial Policy Studies

David A. Weisbach
Visiting Scholar

Paul Wolfowitz
Visiting Scholar

John Yoo
Visiting Scholar

Benjamin Zycher
NRI Visiting Fellow

ALSO AVAILABLE FROM COMMON SENSE CONCEPTS:

Wealth and Justice: The Morality of Democratic Capitalism
by Peter Wehner and Arthur C. Brooks

In *Wealth and Justice: The Morality of Democratic Capitalism*, Peter Wehner and Arthur C. Brooks explore how America's system of democratic capitalism both depends upon and cultivates an intricate social web of families, churches, and communities. Far from oppressing and depriving individuals, the free market system uniquely enables Americans to exercise vocation and experience the dignity of self-sufficiency, all while contributing to the common good. The fruits of this system include the alleviation of poverty, better health, and greater access to education than at any other time in human history—but also a more significant prosperity: the flourishing of the human soul.

Boom and Bust: Financial Cycles and Human Prosperity
by Alex J. Pollock

In *Boom and Bust: Financial Cycles and Human Prosperity*, Alex J. Pollock argues that while economic downturns can be frightening and difficult, people living in free market economies enjoy greater health, better access to basic necessities, better education, work less arduous jobs, and have more choices and wider horizons than people at any other point in history. This wonderful reality would not exist in the absence of financial cycles. This book explains why.

To order a copy of these titles or for information on how you can include Common Sense Concepts in your classroom please visit commonsenseconcept.com